OF DUST AND STARS

Of Dust and Stars

SELECTED POEMS

by

Vernon Ward

EXPOSITION PRESS   NEW YORK

The following poems included in this selection were copyrighted by Vernon Ward in 1949:
Jails and Gallows, I Am Not Patriotic, What Is to Conform?, Tradition Totters, People Are People, Wiping Out Color, Sky Writing, Faith, Quietly Munching an Apple, To Certain New Yorkers, Black Man of the Plow, Cherokee Tragedy, Marie's Day, Chief Engineer, To Ananioski, My Friend, New Pioneering, Hunger, Oh, Stolen Away, Trivia, A Spark Once Struck, Of the Spring, The Soul, Bottle on a Stump, Man May Not Crease the Sea, Mechanitalis: Giant Beyond Reason, Of Time's Eternity, Of Violets, There Were Trees, When You Plant a Tree, Celebration, Loneliness at Night, Love Knows One Law, Love's Discovery, Man Mystery, Some Day, Two Sofas, Two Teacups, What More Can Be Said About Love?, God Is Love, A mon ami, A ma chérie, Jamais, Souvenir de Louis, Souvenir de Toi, and Afterthought.

EXPOSITION PRESS INC., 386 Fourth Avenue, New York 16, N.Y.

FIRST EDITION

I gathered the scattered violets,
meaning them for Libby . . .

Contents

PART SIX

OF DUST AND STARS

DEDICATION

I shall not enslave myself.
I must be free
To see with unprejudiced eyes,
To speak the truth fearlessly.
I must not be deflected from my course.
My life, my living, my idling, my wandering
Are for one purpose:
To know the truth and speak it,
To see beauty and reveal it.

PART ONE

I Await the News

I await the news each day
In hope
That there will be some dramatic change
Of policy.

Each day I hope to hear
That the United States and Soviet Russia
Have become friends,
That they, and all the nations,
Have decided against war and weapons,
And plan to devote all power
To creation;
That all the magnificent machines of man,
And all the science and sweat of man,
Are to be employed
For the common good.

Each day I hope to hear
That the rich have decided
To throw their wealth
Into the common pool
For the good of all;
That all men are to be created equal;

That, loving neighbor as self,
Men are to want for neighbor as for self,
To get for neighbor as for self,
To share the burdens of our common society

According to ability,
And to share the benefits
Equally with all.

Each day I seek some sign
That greed, vanity, and hate
Are to be dissolved in love,
And that kindness to one another
Is to reign throughout the planet.

Each day I seek some sign
That no man is to exalt himself
Above his brother;
That none is to be subject to another;
That the heritage of the past,
The creation of the present,
And the possibilities of the future,
Are to be every baby's birthright.

Each day I hope to hear
That nations, classes, races, creeds,
Are to merge into brotherhood;
That the whole earth is to be
Our common neighborhood;
That burdens,
Lightened by science
And shared by all,
Are to be short and sweet;
That production shared by all
Is to be abundant;
That leisure shared by all
Is to give each human soul
Undreamed of freedom
To pursue its own individuality,
To follow its own inclination;
That all may be free
To wander at will

Over the face of the planet
Exchanging greetings with kindly friends
Of every color and clime,
Meeting nothing but friends,
And seeing the spark of love
In every human eye.

Though ten thousand days disappoint me,
I hope
That good will prevail,
And all men will embrace forever
In unbreakable bonds of love.

Each day I await the news.

The End of the Earth

The end of the earth
Did not come as expected.
Instead,
First, the food gave out;
Then, the clothing gave out;
Next, the houses fell down.
One by one, the factories closed,
And, at length,
Even the distilleries and bomb factories
Ceased operation.
Soon after, the last automobile
Coughed its last cough.
Finally,
As the last human gasped his last breath,
A gust of wind came,
And the entire planet was enveloped,
The atmosphere was dense,

And even the unmanned (thus harmless) bombs and rockets
Were covered
With great dunes
Of man's ultimate creation—
Countless tatters of paper.

We Are Doing the Blasting

No need to cry to God:
We are doing the blasting,
Having set our own great power,
Throbbing, humming, shining power,
Our growing, new-discovered power,
Upon ourselves destructively.

So dying by our own hands,
By our own folly,
Victims of our own stupidity,
To whom shall we address our tears?

No need to turn to the heavens:
We ourselves can master our own creation,
Tune it,
Tame it,
Channel it,
Make it hum new melodies,
Weave new harmonies.

We can engineer this power
To build freedom and abundance
For the last living soul,
To build an earth of affection and hearty handshakes,
To build an earth of smiles.

No need to cry out in agony:
We are doing the blasting.
We can stop.

The Positive Side

Fifty billion dollars a year for war,
And more if war comes.
Five hundred billion dollars in ten years,
Fourteen thousand dollars for every American family,
And perhaps fifty thousand dollars for every American family
If it really is war:
The price that America is paying.

If it really is war,
Slaughter and blood,
Destruction and chaos,
Charred bodies by the millions
And death,
Death to the rich
And death to the poor,
Death to the guilty
And death to the innocent,
Indiscriminate death
On a charred and blasted planet.

Let's get on the positive side!
Fifty billion dollars a year for peace,
Five hundred billion dollars in ten years,
Fourteen thousand dollars more for every American family,
A lovely home and garden for every American family,
Comfortable furnishings,
Modern equipment,

For every American,
For the last and least living American.

And why not the fifty thousand a family
That real war would cost?
Five thousand dollars a year
For every American family
More than it is already getting!

Instead of the waste and blood of war,
Shall we not, for the same price, lift up America's poorest
        infant
To comfort and abundance?

No slaughter and blood, friends.
No destruction and chaos.
No charred bodies.
For we can have, at no greater cost,
Lovely homes and gardens,
New industries and enterprises,
Swamps drained,
Deserts watered,
Forests restored,
Soil reclaimed,
Life sustained,
Abundance for everyone forever.

We have been paying for heaven
And getting hell.
Let's get heaven!
Yes, friends,
Yes!
Let's get on the positive side.

Countergreed Is Not the Answer to Greed

I once thought
That the wrath of the oppressed
Was just,
But too often
The slave has risen
And enslaved the master,
And oppression has been re-established
In reverse.

Countergreed
Is not the answer to greed.
The oppressed should not oppress the oppressor.
He should love the oppressor,
Forgive the oppressor,
Be kind to the oppressor.
He who has suffered the pain of oppression
Knows this pain
And should not inflict such agony on others,
Not even on the oppressor.

Countergreed is not the answer to greed.
Vengeance is not justice,
And hate cannot build brotherhood.
Only the love that embraces, forgives,
And is kind to all mankind
Is the answer to greed.
The good life comes,
Not through the struggle of classes,
But through the merging of classes
Into classlessness
Because of love.
Equality will never be established
Except by love.

Everyone to His Taste

"Everyone to his taste,"
Doctor Rabelais engraved
Above the entrance to his hospital.

For Doctor Rabelais realized
That every man, woman, and child
Generated on earth,
Like every tree or grain of sand,
Is different.

Different inwardly and outwardly,
Different in appearance,
Different in feelings,
And there can never be happiness
Until the last human deviation is recognized
And the last human yearning is fulfilled.

Unless we know what the other wants
We cannot know what the other should have,
For not what we think he should have,
But what he thinks he should have,
He should have.

Appeal

To man, the mighty creature
Who holds atomic power,
Who hurtles off to Venus
At any unseen hour,
Who now may seize the impulse
That drives the potent sun,

Whose dawn of discovery
Has hardly yet begun:
To him give strength of muscle
To mate his fertile mind;
And love and life eternal
Grant him force to find.

So
May this be the foretaste
Rather than the end
Of muscle, nerve and sinew,
Of steel that cannot bend,
Of pulse that surges forward,
Of sense that cannot spend,
Soaring without climax,
Rising without a fall
To a vital fellowship
Permeating all.

I Was Once a Member

I was once a member
Of an exclusive fraternity
To which Du Ponts themselves belonged.
But many of the most delightful people I met
Were outside the fraternity.

I once belonged to a literary society,
But many of our greatest writers
Belonged to no literary society
And gained fame late in life,
Or after death,
Or not at all.

I once belonged to a scientific institute,
But the greatest scientists
Were lonely souls
Disowned by all scientific institutes.

I once belonged to a church,
But most of the best people I met
Belonged to some other church,
Or some other religion,
Or to none.

So, in the end,
I decided to retain membership
In only one society:
Mankind.

Happiness and Unhappiness

In Canada
A boy who released an atom bomb
Grieves in a monastery,
While in USA
An older man
Springs from his jail cell, merry.

One imprisoned himself
By killing.
The killers could not imprison the other,
Who was willing
To risk his life for the salvation
Of his brother.

Up, Man!

Truce in Korea?
Good!
But we must have more than a truce;
We must have peace.

Three million dead?
A thing beyond horror.
But let us forget that;
We can't help that now.
We must get peace.

This must be more than a truce.
No mere cessation of hostilities will do now;
For cataclysm must not be added to horror.
We cannot allow that.

This must be a complete turning
From hate and retribution
To love and creation.
This must be a rededication to life;
A union of east and west;
A merging of class with class,
Religion with religion,
Color with color,
Nation with nation;
A marriage of the individual to humanity
And of humanity to the individual;
A sharp, clean turn
From destroying to building,
From killing to caring.

Down, guns!
Down, tanks, bombers, missiles!
Down, barriers!

Down, race, class, religion, nation, creed!
Down, division and destruction!

Up, houses!
Up, theatres, schools, stadia!
Up, community houses, libraries, parks!
Up, grains, vegetables, fruits!
Up, equality!
Up, unity!
Up, brotherhood, creation, love!
Up, man without color, class, nation!
Up, working, playing, laughing, loving man,
Shoulders erect, head high,
Warm handclasp, no gun . . . .

Up, man!

Return, America!

The United States of America,
Where all men were to have been created equal;
Where there was to have been
Equal opportunity for all,
Special privilege for none;
Where there was to have been
Equal justice under the law;
Where there was to have been
Government of, by, and for the people;
Where there was to have been
Freedom.

Great, broad land,
Land with Atlantic shores and Pacific shores,

Land with Appalachians and Rockies and great plains between,
Land with one hundred and sixty million people
Where wetbacks and Negroes and Du Ponts were to have been
      equal, but are not.
By what incredible margin have we missed our mark?

And now,
1951,
War,
Preparations for war,
Diminishing labor for creation,
Increasing labor for destruction,
Inequality,
Oppression,
Injustice,
War,
More war.

War of, by, and for the mighty
To dominate the planet
As the people slave and perish.
This, my friends,
Is the state of the union.

Equality,
Justice,
Freedom,
Democracy,
The great dream of brotherhood
That was to have been America.

Return, America!

Jails and Gallows

In India
Gandhi went to jail.
Gandhi thought Indians
Should have independence.
He thought it was time
To bring exploitation
By the British
To an end.

The jails were honored by his presence.

Nehru went to jail.
Nehru believed government
Should own industry.
He believed the people should share
The better things of life.

The jails were honored by his presence.

In America
Debs went to jail.
Debs thought peace was a good thing.
When nations were at war
He called for peace.

The jails were honored by his presence.

Thomas went to jail.
Thomas wanted laborers
To have justice.
He said he believed in justice
For the working man.

The jails were honored by his presence.

Gandhi
Brought about the beginning
Of representative government
In India.

Nehru is president
Of the All-Indian Congress.

Debs has forgotten bars
And musty cells.
Debs has found peace.

Thomas is still fighting
For socialism.

The jails were honored by their presence.

There must be a difference, I think,
Between going to jail for killing a man
And going to jail
For saying that laborers should have justice.

Columbus was enchained.
Christ was crucified.
Jails and gallows must be hallowed institutions.

I think it must be good
To go to jail.
So many great men have rested there.

I Am Not Patriotic

I am not patriotic.
I do not believe in America first,
Nor in Japan first,
Nor in Germany first,
Nor in Russia first.
For the least among the nations
I would ask the same as for my own,
The same plenty and peace and happiness
For its people.

I believe that all men are brothers,
That humanity is one family.
I identify myself with Chinamen,
And South Africans,
And New Zealanders,
And Argentinos.
I am all of them.
For the least of human beings
I would ask
The same as for myself,
And more if his need were greater:
Just as much for my brother in India,
And just as much for my brother in Ecuador.

With Tom Paine, I say,
"My country is the world!"
And I am glad to say it.
Any other country
Would be too small.

And I say now
That my brothers should not be killing each other.
Japanese should not be killing Americans,
And Americans should not be killing Japanese.

And Germans should not be killing Russians,
And Russians should not be killing Germans.
They are all fine fellows
When you get to know them;
And I know them well,
For they are all my brothers,
And I am all of them.

This war should not have been
And should not be.
Instead
All of us ought to be building
One world for humanity.

What Is to Conform?

What is to conform
But to fit one's self into a rigid mould,
A common form for earthen pots?
What to conform
But to repress one's self,
To deny one's urges
And to crush the poetry of one's soul?

I want not conformity.
I want individuality,
The freedom to laugh and live and cherish,
The freedom of sun and air and sea,
The freedom of a formless cloud
Blown by the wind
Earthward and seaward.

I want not conformity.
I want the freedom to rove eternally

Regardless of yesterday and today,
Heedless of tomorrow's repentance,
The freedom to rove incessantly,
To bare my foot to all sods,
To bare my back to all suns,
To feel the cool caress of all seas,
To be struck by the lightning of virile love.

Last night I saw a comrade
Cold and rigid, tense and pent-up,
A comrade conforming,
Fitting himself into a painful mould,
Making himself a cog in an obsolete machine
And inactive against its obsolescence.

What are grocery stores to me?
Grocery stores and bank counters,
Coal bins and munitions factories,
Dark cells and sweatshops?
Would I be a grocer or a banker,
A coal seller or a maker of nitrocellulose,
A prisoner or a slave?

Would I fit into any pattern
Of a false society
Of poverty and crime,
Of bondage and idleness,
Of fighting, backbiting
And greedy competition?

Rather would I be free, creative,
An inventor, pioneer,
A dreamer dreaming of a new day
When old shams and tabus will be discredited
And men will live unhampered
And in beauty on the earth.

Rather would I discredit old tabus
By not regarding them,
By living as I long to live,
Loving all men
And hating none,
Loving all soils
And bound to none,
Evanescent and unfettered.

Rather let me be
The first citizen of a new world
Where all men are friends and comrades
Planning together to use inventor's skill
To set men free from their slavery.

For what is to conform
But to repress one's self,
To deny one's urges
And to crush the poetry of one's soul?

Tradition Totters

Youth never fears
To upset dead tradition.
Bravely treads he unknown ways
And flirts with dread perdition.
So gaily lives the youth his days,
And actively his years.

Why of this and how of that?
The earth endures inspection.
And weakness here or weakness there
Is not beyond detection.

33

He questions all and everything.
Behold! He questions boldly.
Because it is and because it was
Are answers he takes coldly.

Is it in the Constitution?
Or rule imposed by Puritan?
So much the more its destitution
Of reason known to modern man.
Does pot hold water now, today?
If not, then throw the pot away.
None he'll have of outworn pot,
For ancient pot is not, he'll say,
Exactly what he'd mould today.

And so: Until new sons arise
To upset dead tradition,
To bravely tread the unknown ways
And flirt with dread perdition.

People Are People

Catholic, Protestant, Mohammedan, Jew,
You're for me, I'm for you;
Rich man great, poor man small,
People are people, that's all.

The Chinaman through the darkness slinking
Just put a dollar in the beggar's cup.
That slithering dame who passed you winking
Will this night with a senator sup.
One may rise, another may fall,
But people are people, that's all.

The black lumberjack with muscles great,
The kid on the corner waiting for his date,
The football player running to cheers,
The poor old widow shedding her tears:
They all have feelings, their hopes and their fears,
The same love of home, the same dream of peace
As the ragged wharf rat in Nice.
O, you may plow, you may pitch a ball,
But people are people, that's all.

Black African or red-bearded Afghan,
Slant-eyed native of Turkestan,
Hollywood Boulevard American,
Regardless of color, of fortune or name,
The pulse beat is human, the blood is the same.
From jungle sweat, from mountain tall,
People are people, that's all.

Each man feels the warmth of the sun.
Muscle and flesh and love are one.
Brother and sister, sister and brother,
Each is as good as any other.
In icy northwood, glittering hall,
People are people, that's all.

Catholic, Protestant, Mohammedan, Jew,
Capitalist, Communist, Atheist too,
Rich man great, poor man small,
People are people, that's all.

Wiping Out Color

I sent a letter to a Southern paper.
Two things I wrote they censored:
"The best solution to the race question
Is to forget race."
And "Nothing wipes out color faster than friendship."

Nobody censors here:
The best solution to the race question
Is to forget race.
Nothing wipes out color faster than friendship.

Sky Writing

Have you ever seen a meteor
Hurled across the sky?
I am going to show you one.
Maybe you'll get some of its tail
Caught in your eye.

America is great, you say.
And you are right.
America is greater than Kokomo,
And greater than Chicago,
Greater than Virginia or New Mexico.
But you were born a generation too late.
We now must take the world in tow.

It's great to be an American, you say.

And I agree with you.
It's greater to be an American

Than a hooter of Podunk Center,
Or a booter of the Great White Way,
Or a crying California patriot.
But it's also good to be a Mexican,
And just as fine to be an Afghan,
Or a turbaned Sikh of Hindustan.
In fact,
It's very nice
To be any kind of a man.

Being American is not enough.
Man is made of bigger stuff.
We now meet China face to face
And take the world in our embrace.

I'm not born too soon,
Not gazing at the stars,
At Venus and Mars,
Nor even at the moon.
This song will soon be obsolete.
We'll sing to music twice as sweet,
Though still incomplete.
Man will dash through asteroids
Discovering that the boundless voids
Aren't so void
After all.

It's not a question, friend, of years
That dims your eye with tears.
It's only what you see.
Come have a look with me:

Have you ever seen a meteor
Brightly flashing by?
If you catch the faintest gleam
It claims your very eye.
It cannot leave the sky,

37

My friend,
It cannot leave the sky.
And never can it die.

Faith

What faith man has!
Out of a thousand ruins,
Above a million defeats,
He rises clear eyed,
Grasping for victory.

Of War And Love

War is love's essence lost.
Think of young men
Killed in their prime,
Of tense, urgent loins
Flaccid with fatigue,
Their recrudescent passion spent
In murder and destruction
Without recrudescence.

Think of children
Starved to impotence
Before puberty,
Of mothers gaping
With babes in their wombs,
Of men away from their women,
Of females divested of their males.

And all to what end
But fratricide,
The devastation
Of the love nests of nations,
The wringing of fledglings' necks?

I have heard
That too much love
Is wasted effort.
How about too much war?

Is not effort
To destroy love,
To promote starvation, misery, murder,
To lay lands waste,
All the more wasted;
And far more than wasted?

Think of men
Straining backs,
Tensing leg muscles,
Surging to slaughter,
When they might embrace one another.

The very men
Who stab one another
Might far better enfold one another
In passionate encirclement
And rise with renewed vigor
To return to a thousand fresh embraces
In a multitude of happy climes.

How much better
To love than to hate,
To kiss than to kill.

If all the crucial force
Mustering to war
Were pulsing to passion,
There would be no end to love.

Love Without End

For all mankind
Love must be free,
Unashamed,
At will
And by mutual impulse.

Disease must be conquered
To make the earth
Safe for love.

Love must be the cohesive force
Uniting humanity
Into a oneness
Without hate,
Without fear,
Without greed:
Into a universal nirvana.

There will be no end
To love.

PART TWO

Quietly Munching an Apple

As I sit here in my room
Quietly munching an apple,
What is happening on Fifth Avenue?
And what is happening on Times Square?

I am in a room.
The walls are bare.
There are a bed and bureau,
A table and two chairs.
And I am sitting at the table
Quietly munching an apple.

Oh, yes,
I hear rumors of outside traffic,
Occasionally the grating of a train on the el-track,
Sometimes the sputter of a plane overhead,
Or the throaty blast of a ship at harbor.

All around me are rooms,
Millions of rooms,
Mostly dark now,
For New Yorkers have not begun seeking their privacy.
They are on Fifth Avenue
And on Times Square
Dashing madly,
Or staring crazily;
Or assembled in big rooms

To worship idols
Or hear music.

As I sit here in my room
Quietly munching an apple,
What is happening in China?
And what is happening in Spain?

To Certain New Yorkers

1.

Milady, no need to hide your face from me.
No need to pull down your hat brim.
Who are you anyway?
A great actress,
Afraid I want your autograph?
A hunted criminal,
Afraid I'll detect you?
An heiress or a prostitute?

I wouldn't have looked at you
If you'd stared me full in the face.
And even if I had looked at you,
I wouldn't have known you.
Why should you be conscious of me?
Who am I that you should hide from me?

I caught a glimpse of your pale throat,
And I think I've seen many a country lass
Of straw colored hair and brown skin
Whose clear blue eyes I'd much prefer
To those you hid from me.

2.

You, Esquire,
Standing there in front of the Waldorf.
Apparently you have the world at your feet.
And apparently you know it.
Alexander the Great, Caesar and Napoleon
Would probably be your footmen.
Tell me, Esquire,
Do you own all of these towers?
Or are they merely your minarets?
Now, Colossus or Philaster,
Or perhaps it's better to say Pilaster,
For you are one of the pillars of the State
(That's why the edifice is condemned),
Who are you anyway?

3.

So you are wearing orchids,
Three of them!
They are lovely,
But so perishable!
The fellow walking beside you
Bought them, I suppose.
Sort of dough-faced, isn't he?
And your face looks fagged out too.
The orchids are lovely,
But your face is all in a rash.
What is it, Miss? Indigestion?

Watch out, Miss!
Don't stumble over that man
On the sidewalk.

4.

Now, honestly,
It may have been your face I saw,

But it looked to me
More like a mask.
I don't mean to say
The lips weren't perfectly shaped,
But they looked to me like red paint.
And I don't mean to say
The eyes weren't incredibly blue,
But where'd you find the dark circles?
And do you mean to tell me
You got that suntan at the beach?

Well, I didn't see your fingernails,
So I can't say anything definite
About them,
But I think I know how they look.

Someday you'll get hair dye
And false teeth.

Black Man of the Plow

Ankle deep in new turned loam
He tramps down endless rows.
Like a knotted, gnarled gnome
Timelessly he goes.
Grime upon his ankles black
He moves with measured pace.
Wet the rags upon his back.
Streaming wet his face.

Little knows he of the earth,
Of how its surface turns.
Little knows he money's worth,

Little money earns.
He never thinks of latest styles;
Nor hears of pacts unsealed.
He hardly knows ten other miles
Than those within his field.

He knows the mule and knows the plow.
He knows the summer sun.
He knows the smell of dung and mow,
And knows when day is done.
He knows to sing in harmony
With family folk and friends
A southern summer rhapsody
That lazily ascends.

To smile a flashing smile he knows,
To feel with feeling deep.
And while the world still madly goes
He knows in peace to sleep.
He is the black man of the plow,
Barefoot, walking languidly,
Who never cares for past or now,
Nor wonders at futurity.

Cherokee Tragedy

No arrow he fashioned could shoot more swiftly
Than his body forged in ripstream line.
No mocassin he made could patter more lightly
Than his velvet foot over carpet of pine.
No mouse or squirrel could steal more softly
Than his shadowed form through bramble and vine.
No creeper or moss could cling more deftly
Than his facile hand to canyon incline.

In the barroom he howled like a hound,
And his throat strings knotted with strain.
And he shouted at cronies and mongrels
A roaring volley profane.
His sharp angered eye flashed blackly
At the innocent cur who would fain
Steal to bed his half-breed,
And quick cocked fist shot pain.

The crashing of a land cave,
The wrecking rush of storm lave,
The pounding of a tide wave,
His power spent its throb.
Like falcon's form at far flight,
Like sea spray struck by sunlight,
Like music sung at midnight,
His beauty spent its sob.

Marie's Day

Marie's eyes opened.
Her hand rubbed her black body
Extended in the sunrise.
Her arms stretched back.
Her waist twisted.
Her body turned over.
Her eyes closed.

(She felt a hand on her back,
Felt it pull her dress down
Over her hips,
Felt it shake her.)
She turned over.

It was Mammy.
She got off the bed.

Slowly she walked out the back door
To the woodpile,
Picked up the axe,
Got it over her shoulder,
Dropped it heavily
To the knotty wood.
She picked up an armful
Of the wood,
Stumbled into the cookshack,
Let the wood clatter to the floor.

She stood there looking at her Mammy,
Who mixed corn meal,
And water,
And salt;
Stood there looking at her Mammy's rags,
At the jelly of her Mammy's arms,
Of her Mammy's legs.

She stretched her legs
Under the greasy table,
Spread her feet apart,
Poured molasses from a half-gallon
Into her cracked plate.
She took salty bacon
From the pan
With her fingers.
She pushed cornbread
Through the molasses,
Saw the brown plate,
Saw the brown molasses
Cover the brown plate.
She poked cornbread into her mouth,

Chewed,
Swallowed heavily.
She saw her brothers sopping molasses,
And her Mammy,
And her Grandmammy.

She held greasy pans,
Plates,
Rusty cups,
Spoons,
In hot water
That ran out through a hole
In the bottom of the pan.
She squeezed lye soap
Through her fingers.

The farm bell rang.

She kicked dust along the road
To the tobacco field.
She waded through hot sand
Into the field
And with the other Negroes on the farm
Pulled out the suckers
That grow between the stalk
And the leaf,
Sucker after sucker,
Row after row.

(She felt the gummy, wilted suckers
Between her fingers,
Felt the sweat
Itching down her back.
She smelt the dust.
She looked at men working,
Their bare backs
Streaked with sweat,

Wide and strong,
Muscular and shiny;
At the hard thighs
Under blue cloth,
Thighs stronger than her big brother's.
She felt weak inside.)

She pulled the wet cloth
Out from her middle
And worked on,
Sucker after sucker,
Row after row.

The farm bell rang.

She walked dripping to the shack,
Sat down at the table
With her brothers,
And her Mammy,
And her Grandmammy,
Ate collard greens,
Salty pork,
Cold corn bread.

She followed her brothers
Running
To the creek
Behind the field
Where the young ones swam
And the old ones lay around
After dinner
In the cypress shade
Looking at the young ones.

She waded into the creek,
Splashed the sluggish water.
Her feet oozed into mud.

49

(She felt the hot water
Against her skin,
Felt the hands of the older boys
And the stronger hands of men
Throw her into the slime,
Heard their laughter.)

The farm bell rang.

With the others
She walked through summer sand
To the field,
The mud caked on her ankles,
Cracked.
The slime dried on her back,
Drew her skin tight.
She looked at the Negro men
Working in the field,
At the wet cloth
Taut over their buttocks
As they bent to the suckers.
She rubbed her back
With her gummy hand,
Saw the sun
Hung above the trees.
She worked on,
Sucker after sucker,
Row after row.

The farm bell rang.

Through the dusk
She staggered to the shack,
Dropped to the ground
In the yard
Beneath the big oak tree,

Rubbed a mosquito
Off her face,
Stretched her arms
Behind her head,
Drew a deep breath
Of sultry air.

When her Mammy called
She went inside,
Sopped molasses,
Saw the others sop.

Her body bent over the dishpan.
Her hands wiped out pans,
Plates,
Cups,
Spoons.
Her legs trembled.

She heard thunder.
She fell into bed
With her brothers,
Close to her big brother,
Buried her nose in the straw mattress.

(She felt her big brother
Rubbing up against her,
Felt his strong arm around her.)

She turned over,
Drew breath sharply.

(She heard the quick beat of rain
On the shingles,
Felt drops of it on her face,
On her legs,
On her big brother's back.

She smelt a steam of ancient urine
Rising from the mattress.)

Marie's eyes closed.

Chief Engineer

Let me laugh at this man.
On this ship he is Chief Engineer.
And yet
He can hardly totter.
Khaki clad and grizzled,
He looks as if he had known
A century of debauchery,
As if he carried the full weight
Of man's degeneracy
On his shoulders.

What storms has his body known?
Wracked by syphilis and gonorrhea,
Sluggish from a thousand nights
In a multitude of taverns,
He stands looking at the sea,
Each eye working independently
In its putty socket.

And the puffing!
He never removes the cigarette
From his palsied lips,
Never lifts a hand,
Never tauts a muscle.
Day after day he stands there
Drooping at the rail,
Looking at the sea gulls.

To Ananioski

Ananioski,
May the Great Mystery
Of all good people
Grant me words to express
My great love for you.
May all the yokes and shackles of man
Be broken.
May my heart be freed
To soar as the eagle soars
To the altar of the Cherokees
To be embedded in your soul.

Ananioski,
Today you are gone.
This morning the tide ebbed
And swept you away from me.
And today I feel
As if the greater part of myself
Had been severed from me,
As if my soul had left me.

Ananioski,
How much do I love you!
How often have I said
Ananioski whom I love more than I love myself!
Ananioski for whom I would gladly die!
Can I ever say Ananioski
Without saying
Whom I love more than I love myself?
It is part of my name for you.

Ananioski,
When I see your face,
Bronze, rigid,
When I see your face relaxed,

Lips slightly parted,
Iron nose of the Cherokee,
Eyes brown, warm, friendly,
When I see your face fill with love,
Your lips warm to a smile,
Your eyes glow with affection:
Your face lights my heart
As the moon lights the sea.

And your body,
Ananioski,
With its great muscles flowing
Under satin skin,
Its broad chest,
Sculptured shoulders,
Powerful arms,
Slim waist,
Sharp-muscled legs,
Is more beautiful to me
Than all the statues of Greece.

But my love for your body,
Ananioski,
And your face,
Is as a grain of sand
To my love for the life and soul of you,
For the spirit
That makes your eyes gleam
And your body move
In the way of the good Indian.
Your faith, your trust, your loyalty, your love
Are a part of the Great Mystery itself.

Ananioski,
Can you ever know
The true depth of my feeling
Which is greater than the depth of the Universe?

Words are broken arrows.
They cannot reach their mark.

But Ananioski,
The Great Mystery has looked upon our love
And regarded it with favor.
He has brought us together
And made us friends.
He has watched over us
As I became part of you,
As you became part of me,
As the essence of your life
Became the essence of my life.
The Great Mystery has sealed us together
Forever.

And Ananioski,
When we come to the last council ring,
And sitting there under the pines and the moon
Smoking together the final pipe of peace,
Watching in silence
The smoke rising from our pipe
And the smoke rising from the embers
Of the council fire,
Watching until we ourselves
Go up with the smoke
To the Great Mystery,
May we rise together,
Ananioski,
To hunt in the last of all hunting grounds,
The Happy Hunting Ground,
Forever.

My Friend

The combine motor broke down.
How quick to act you were!
You asked for the screw driver
And tried the spark.
"Fire's okay," you snapped.
Then
With a little wrench
Your dexterous hands
Disconnected the gas line.
Cheeks puffed out,
You blew out the trash.
The couplings were back
As quick as a flash.
Then
Taking off the gas cap
You blew into the tank.
The rim left a black circle
Around your mouth.
The motor started
At your whip of the crank,
And we were whisking through the wheat again.

As You Are, My Friend

If I were a cripple,
As you are, my friend,
I would never see the waterfront
Different than now;
But would sit here at my window,
Day after day,
And see in the distance

56

The trawlers creeping along
And the tugs drawing their barges by.

If I were a cripple,
As you are, my friend,
I would never walk
Down among the warehouses
And across the railroad tracks
And onto the piers,
Never see the darkies sweating
And rolling cargo,
Or the bilge of ships,
Or by night
The solitary woman
Unobtrusively wearing out her shoe soles.

But all the same
I would sit here at my window,
As you do, my friend,
Seeing the waterfront spread out wide
And washed of its filth.
And I would be happy
Watching the trawlers
Out at sunrise
And in at sunset,
And seeing the sails
Silver by moonlight.

And come stormy weather,
I would paint the fog
With my dreams.

You—Plus Love

Now I see it can never be,
For I love you; you don't love me.
And all the wishing that I may do
Can never change what's really true.

You can't help what's in your heart.
Love isn't made by whim or art.
You feel one way, I another.
I'm your lover; you're my brother.

Brotherhood, beloved, isn't enough.
Love reaches out for equal stuff.
Still
One combination I couldn't improve:
You again—plus love.

PART THREE

Of Dust and Stars

Of dust and stars
Man is made,
Of glowing sun
And secret shade,
Of dismal depth
And towering height,
Of weakness faint
And magic might.

Man is made
Of dust and stars,
Of freedom wide
And crippling bars,
Of tender kisses,
Jolts and jars.
A mortal soul
Of stars and dust,
Bound to earth,
Yet rise he must.

Who on earth
Can yet compare
Such potent strength
And frailty rare?
Throughout the stars
What mind could think
A soaring angel
So low could sink?

Body chained,
Head held high,
Feet on earth,
Eyes in the sky.
His finite spirit
Will not fade.
Of dust and stars
Man is made.

New Pioneering

I know what there is to know
Of the earth.
I have not lived my life
In books.
I have not lived my life
In dreams.
I have sent my body forth
To accept the offerings
Of the earth.

Nothing have I feared.
Boldly have I followed
Forbidden pathways,
Boldly trespassed
Forbidden grounds.
Forbidden forests
I have found beautiful.

I have undertaken
New pioneering.

Hunger

Stretched out warmly under stars,
Lulled by breeze and weaving sea,
Serenaded by the palms,
I have kept my reverie.
I have slept on lonely bars,
Mind and body, quietly,
Stretched out warmly under stars,
And still could sleep there endlessly.

In ivy-covered walls I've lived
And heard the bells ring out,
Have trod the shaded campus ways
To classroom and about,
Have fondly held Arabian Nights
And drawn of Byron's breath,
But never found satiety
Of life, or love, or death.

I have known Hawaiian skies,
Have felt that golden sun;
And though I long lay under it
My longing was not done.

I have seen proud Notre Dame
And walking in its door
Have caught my breath in startlement
That gripped me to the core,
By moonlight seen the Taj Mahal
In marble pool reflected;
Rising white like ivory,
Its spirit I've detected.

With aching legs and burning eyes
Himalaya snows I've faced
Mounting high the hidden ways

To distances unpaced,
Deep in forests of stately fir
Beside the River Sind,
Between the mountains crystalline
That secret haunts defend.
And now afar from Zoji La,
My memory is fond
Of dwelling on the gothic wall
And in the lands beyond.

Again, I know of mule and plow,
Of dawn and setting sun.
Again, I know where fields are wide
And idle rivers run.
The feel of axe and hoe I know,
The smell of sweat and dung.
And yet the lure is ever strong,
And yet the song's unsung.

In all of seven seas I've swum,
In Carolina mountain stream,
And diving in an emerald pool
I've seen the waters gleam,
But still of waters dream.

And then, the shining seas I've sailed,
And then, the stormy seas,
But never yet has my heart failed
In calmest sea or breeze
To desire a farther shore,
Onward roving ever,
To know the mystery and the store
Held by distant land before
And for its wealth to fever.

Mohamad's mullah showed me once
Islamia's magic spell,

And Buddha's ancient incense
My spirit did compel;
Then, I have sipped at Vishnu's well,
Can Brahma's story tell,
But still I want the somber toll
Of holy Christian bell.

I have drunk from Venus' cup,
Have tasted Bacchus' wine,
And lain a while at Omar's side
To celebrate the vine.
All the essences of life,
All the nectars sweet,
The smell of summer flowers,
The touch of Eros' heat,
The misty veil of moonlight,
Within my soul compete
And leave me with a hunger
That nothing can complete.

I still am thirsting after life
To know the secrets of the soul,
To drink my fill at every stream
And tread where radiant thunders roll.
I want to marry the fallow earth,
To intermingle with its soil,
To give myself new, fertile birth
For roving, life and love and toil.

O, thus I must complete myself
And thus must find the sheen
Of all the richest things on earth
That are or yet have been.

Oh, Stolen Away

The fire still burns
In the big fireplace,
But my cabin no longer is home.
The gun still hangs
Above the door,
But the one thing of beauty is gone.

Indian blankets
Hang from the logs
As ever they did before.
And etchings and paintings
Adorn yet the walls,
But my cabin no longer is home.

Colorful books
Attend on the shelves,
And the bearskin rests on the floor.
But the antlers can never,
Oh, never replace
The one thing of beauty that's gone.

Just two days ago
A beautiful painting
Was hanging upon the wall,
Just two days ago
Where antlers now hang.
My cabin no longer is home.

And now it is gone,
Oh, whither? Oh, whither?
Pray, let me see it again.
Someone has stolen
The Silver Spot.
The one thing of beauty is gone.

Oh, many the hour
I sat by my fire
Admiring The Silver Spot.
And many the gloom
I thus did dispell.
My cabin no longer is home.

And now it is stolen,
Oh, stolen away,
And, oh, how I envy the robber!
But I know not who,
And I know not where
My one thing of beauty is gone.

The fire still burns
In the big fireplace,
But my cabin no longer is home.
The gun still hangs
Above the door,
But the one thing of beauty is gone.

Two Cats Make the World

Two cats at play in the periwinkle,
One attacking and one defending,
Pawing each other caressingly,
Rolling and tossing resiliently,
Skipping and tripping on soft-padded feet.
How wary she is!
Always retreating to be alluring,
Never too far and never too fast,
Always turning to watch his advances.
How sage he is!
Always pursuing and tantalizing,

Never aggressive and never impatient,
Always sure in anxious restraint.

The Empire State rises blue in the morning.
The church-tower bell is just striking six.
The trucks rumble past on their endless mission.
In the periwinkle bed two cats make the world.

Trivia

1.

Hiram Jones, of ancient age,
Little knew of birth control.
Now we'd think it hardly sage,
Perhaps a little droll,
If one from ranks of modern youth
Should be a match for Hiram's truth:
Children thirty-six.

2.

Leaping water,
Leaping water,
I am leaping water.
I fall down dashing from the clouds
And speed over mossy rocks,
And when I reach the level plains
I rest in lazy rivers.

3.

With a gay chuckle
The robin makes a red target
In the china tree,

66

Swells big his breast,
Cocks his head.
The child
Drops his air gun.

4.

The moon steals above the trees
And laughs at us.
We are indignant.
The moon turns pale
And hides behind a cloud.

5.

His muscled arms
Hold American industry
Out of chaos.
Bent beneath his burden
Stands the modern worker.

6.

Midst debris he stands
Looking upward
Toward a vision
In the blank blue:
The new youth.

7.

The day sings
Until the night cloud
Chases the amber eve
To the black hills
And bathes us
In dark hush.

8.

Icy diamonds
Drips the night
Into the lantern light.

9.

The tree is less lasting than the forest
Shall we consider the tree
Or the forest?

A Spark Once Struck

A spark once struck never dies,
But catches breath in quick surprise,
Lights in loving human eyes
And makes the startled spirit rise.
The flame that kindles cannot die.
Years may pass, it cannot fly.
It warms each lover to the heart
Forging bonds that cannot part.
Lovers half a world around
Feel its warmth, hear its sound.

Once a handclasp or a kiss
Strikes two souls to earthly bliss,
Nothing then can break the bond
Tied by bodies growing fond.
Removed by spaces or by years,
Beaten down by earthly fears,
Through the struggles and the tears,
All the pulses of the heart
Are the bonds that cannot part.

Love will banish time and space,
Will every barricade erase;
Then shall we meet face to face,
Heal our hurts in warm embrace.
The throbbing heart will speed its beat
When loving human bodies meet.

A million flames may yet awake
And not a single heart forsake.
A spark once struck never dies
But lights forever loving eyes.

Aspiration

Life,
Oh, the glory of it,
The incredible, impossible vaulting of it!
Just a day of this
Would justify all these centuries,
These struggles from caves and jungles,
These long agonies
And dark eons
That kept faith
In hope that some day
Life would be beautiful.

And this endless joy
Is but the beginning
Of what will come.
Shadowed still by dark obstructions
That steal youth's sunlight,
That snuff out the bright spark,
The slow, magnificent, impulsive beat

Of this ardent current,
Beauty yet proves infinite.

Only what expands life
Is good.
And all that endangers life
Is evil.
To make pain cease
And pleasure grow
Is our quest.

For what robs any single soul
Of the richest enjoyment
Of the briefest moment
Of this immortal ecstasy
Is the enemy.
No cloud must touch life's sun,
And any spark once struck
Must be nurtured full to flame,
Never to be extinguished.

This,
And this alone,
Is man aspiration.

The Mating Call

Let me be the one to proclaim
That all love is good
And all hate evil,
That the mating call
Which draws mankind together
Is itself the divinest law,

More divine than all the fatal laws
Which separate man from man.

I do not deny the mating call,
And when it comes
I essay to enter
The sacred realm of love;
For love is the most essential poetry,
The utter crux of life.
And I curse the patterns
Which at times
Have held me apart from my lover.

Love is good for the soul,
And loving enlarges the soul,
But repression consumes the heart of man
And leaves a bitter shell.

Under palm trees or no trees,
Caressed by wafted seaspray,
Out on moonlit beaches,
Beside the moonlit seas,
We have lain together,
My secret love with me,
By love welded together,
To unity welded inseparably.

All of the star-studded towers
Rising above the harbor,
All of the smoke of a thousand stacks,
All of the rumblings of subway trains,
All of the heedless restlessness of the multitude,
I would not have
For one moment
On a moonlit beach
In my lover's arms.

Road for Abiding

You may have the broad highway
With traffic flashing by;
But I would take the country way,
The forest, field and sky.
Give me the dusty way,
The fevered wind's caress,
Where life flows slowly through the day
With sluggish gentleness.

You may choose the traveled road
Where speeding cars careen;
But I would have for my abode
The lonely way, and green.
Give me the quiet road,
The pungent smell of pine,
Where western reds at eve forbode
The sun's intense decline.

Yours may be the glaring lights,
The sound of singing tires;
But mine must be the darksome sights
Where nightbird's song inspires.
Give me the moonlit trail,
The woodland by its side,
Where silver clouds above me sail,
And I will long abide.

PART FOUR

Of the Spring

I sing of the birds in untimed flight,
Of the languid stir of the long leaf pine,
Of the tulips red in the bright sunlight,
Of the golden bells on the jasmine vine.
I sing of the boy who quit the plow,
Who quit his clothes to lie in the sun,
Whose springtime skin is tanning now,
Whose body is lax with lazy fun.

I sing of the madness of the springtime night
When the air is heavy with lilac and song,
When the trees stand black in the red moonlight
And mystery-stream flows rich and strong;
Of the distant voices of the darkies rising
In harmony to the velvet sky;
Of the shadows of the night disguising
The secret soul and the secret sigh.

Of the sun, of the trees, of the sky, I sing,
Of the silver clouds in heaven's arc;
Of the creek, of the fields, of the winds that bring
The hot perfumes and the song of the lark.
Mine is the song of the newborn spring,
Of the greenery bright and the flowers gay;
Of the bells that ring and the birds that sing
Of the sluggish way of a fevered day.

The Soul

A red spark,
A rose glow,
A yellow flame,
An orange coal,
A gray ash.
Where is the soul?

In absolute darkness
Light sparks its cement,
Inspires its flame,
Moulds its child,
Increases it.
Light creates:
Broad shoulders,
Straight back,
Trim waist,
Muscled members,
Clear head,
Penetrating.
These,
Steeped in light,
Cannot know darkness,
Cannot despair.
These defy,
Deny the inevitable,
Live in joy.

The song of the mockingbird
Ascends,
Lives,
Culminates,
Dies.
Where is the soul?

Darkness,
Jealous of light,
Blinded by brilliance,
Corrodes the creation,
Shrivels it.
Darkness destroys:
Stooped shoulders,
Bent back,
Sagging belly,
Inert members,
Cloudy head,
Dull.
These,
Dyed in darkness,
Cannot know light,
Despair,
Surrender to the inevitable.

The amoeba lives,
Divides,
Sacrifices individuality.
But eternally
Lives the amoeba.

Bottle on a Stump

I had just seen a cardinal,
And then I saw
A bottle on a stump.

I looked at the russet carpet of pine,
At the sunrise through the southeast mist,
At the trees thrusting up
And opening their arms

To the blue and white corrugated sky;
And I wondered how anyone could want
A bottle on a stump.

To the Helmsman

Billows of cloud blew overhead
Above the emerald sea,
And rainbows danced in the glittering surf
That dashed across the lee.
The wind was singing a rising song,
And the rigging was a-sway,
And the steady bow was like a plow
That split the waves away.

The sails flapped at the edge of the wind,
And the gulls shrieked at the wake,
And the salty spume burnt our tawny skin
And set the decks a-flake.
The wind wheeled high and the yawl keeled low,
But, lad, it was enow
That you stood staunch at *The Clara's* helm
And I stood at her bow.

Man May Not Crease the Sea

Man may not crease the sea.
Great ships he may build
That ply the waters for a spell,
That stir the waters momentarily in passing;

But the wake fades,
And the sea forgets,
And the swells heave incessantly.

Man may not crease the sea.
His ships may flout the tempest
And spear the highest wave.
But only for a time.
At end the waves ride triumphant.

Changeable is the sea,
Restless, at work eternally.
Some days the work is slow.
The breast hardly heaves.
Blue are the air and the sky,
And the surface flashes sunlight.
Ships come quietly and go quietly,
And the horizon is washed clean.

Changeable is the sea,
Lawless and unreasoning.
Some days the work is fast.
The spume rises and the spray is like smoke.
Black clouds bombard the heavens.
The gulls shriek frantically.
The ships leap
And lose their sharpness in the mist.

For days the sea is empty.
There are nights when stars are ruby and emerald,
When moonrise veils the east with gold,
When cascades of light in the north
Paint the sea with snow.
No man sees,
And the horizon is unblemished.

For days the sea is empty.
The wind claws with icy fingers.
The water slaps and drifts.
Great is the howl and the fury.
Bitter is the cold.
But no man feels,
And the horizon is unblemished.

Changeable is the sea.
Nights of moonlight, nights of starlight,
Nights and days of utter silence,
Days and nights of tropical music.
The power, the frenzy, the impatience
Of great waters always changing,
But changeless to the hand of man.

Man may furrow the earth.
He may fell the forest and loose the soil
And leave the rocks denuded.
He may build clusters of towers
That look as timeless as mountains.
He may close himself in walls
And wallow out of the air and sun.

Man may furrow the earth.
He may build great bridges
Which time turns to rust.
He may soar above the earth
To struggle, rob and kill.
He may cover the earth with his debris,
Leave mounds of eroded metal
To be devoured by water, wind and time.

But man may not crease the sea.
The sea of the Greeks
Is the sea of the Vikings,
And the sea of the Vikings

Is the sea of the Normans,
And ten thousand ships in passing
Leave a clear horizon.

Man may furrow the earth,
But he may not crease the sea.

Mechanitalis: Giant Beyond Reason

1. Has disfigured the earth;

Weighting the heavy gravel
Drums of brazen slime,
Sprayed on the gum of metal
Through the space in time.

Circles of bouncing notches,
Energy divested of men;
Back to death for the living
Racing from life again.

Kettles of hazy glow
Heating into the night.
Banging of mingled twist
Filling air with bite.

Intestinal circumventing iron
Brown from span long hard.
Out with waves of feel
Sluggish with certain retard.

Spikes of grim dull steel.
All of their holy smoke.
Heavenward their sickly mouths
Vomit their fumes of stoke.

79

2.   Has deformed man;

A sage could see the clouds,
Could hear the roaring sky,
But would not dare to understand
The breaking of reply.

There was the red who saw,
Who showed the steam of gray,
Who heeded still unheard:
A hearing would convey.

Slick is the top of the thicket
Crowned with yellow of age.
Up with the wool of the ball.
Away from the blackness of rage!

High the inverted cup,
Bored the peering of eyes.
Furrowed the plateau of wisdom.
Contempt in a language of lies.

Dark from the soot of the digging,
Dulled from the in and the out.
Chattering much, but not sounding.
Having of all, but without.

3.   Has clouded thought;

Rhythmless drumbeat of thought,
Pounding of aching blood.
Infinite conception of life,
Rich (with oozing of mud.)

Packed the cloths of stupor
Numbered in endless rows,
Rowed in endless numbers,
Loaded with loudest of blows.

Hope for the black of passing.
Desire for the undesired.
Fight for the last of shaking,
Point from the blackness fired.

Black the night of day
Extensive to the right.
The energy of white on black:
Merely a trick of sight.

4.   Has crazed action.

Flying feeling of rushing,
Aimless wish of the go,
Wrapped in metals of power,
Out to the wonder of fro.

Bouncing bags of jelly
Patting soul on floor.
Fire of heat devouring
Pollution of the whore.

Into the juicy piping
Slop the drunken hold.
Twisting and churning grip
Pushing toward the cold.

Out beyond the asteroids,
Prying, searching eye.
Back to hell tomorrow,
But top to verify.

Avaunt, Mechanitalis!
Nevermore be seen.
Than the haunt of rattles,
Rather the gust of green.
And than the soft of daily,
Rather the lowly lean.

Of Time's Eternity

Sometimes, in tomes,
For long hours I have leaned over volumes
Seeking the secret
Of time's eternity.
And through the endless procession of pages,
Yellowed,
Sere,
Have despaired.

Sometimes I think
The butterfly momentarily on wing,
Or the drop of dew that in the morning
Moistens the iris' throat
Knows more than I;
For such are briefer born
Of time's eternity.

Of Violets

Now
Shall I pause to speak
Of violets
After these eons of struggle?

It was a simple thing:
Today,
A rainy day in April,
I went to milk the cow
In the sparkling rye.
I led her to the edge
Of an ancient wooded graveyard

Where she might find shelter
For the night.
And there I saw the purple,
The violets,
The heart-shaped leaves,
The scalloped blooms
Beneath the budding trees.

As I gathered the scattered violets,
Meaning them for Libby,
I thought of all the years
When violets must have bloomed unseen,
Trampled down by warring men.

If men should die
At the Dardanelles,
Would not the violets bloom?
If atoms showered
The crumbling earth,
Would not the violets bloom?

That faint odor
Of violets
Seems so sweet
Today.

There Were Trees

Blocks and blocks we walked
Arm in arm
Under the elevated,
And we did not find it drab:
There were thousands of people around
All filled with hearts and nerve and wonder.

83

"Some places they have palm trees,"
I remember saying,
"But then,
Those places they don't have el tracks."

We looked up
And saw the moon
Somewhere
In the ribbon of blue-black sky
Between the roofs and the el tracks

And also
There were stars
Peering through the dark steel framework.

And,
Hand in hand,
Didn't we talk about the relativity of the stars:
How the street lamps looked bigger
Because they were closer,
When the stars were really other suns
With other planets
And other people, maybe?

And then,
After those unverdant
Blocks and blocks,
We saw a little park
And there were trees.

When You Plant a Tree

When you plant a tree
You do not always stay
To see it grow each day.
Sometimes you let it be.

And yet, as time goes by,
You nurture it,
And prune it,
And see its leaves mount high
Reaching for the sky.

It may be some day
That even for a year or more
You may go away
And then come back to see
The greatness of your tree.
Never can your heart ignore
The greenness of your tree.

When you plant a baby tree,
It doesn't always have to be
In your own dark soil.
It may well be for all to see
That you sweat and toil.

Through All Eternity

In body, mind and spirit
I am with you,
And will be
Today, tomorrow and forever.
No matter how soon,
How late,
When you come
I shall be waiting.
If you never come,
I shall still be waiting.
On earth,
After earth,
Always,
My prayer goes with you.
Body of my body,
Blood of my blood,
Soul of my soul,
May love bless you
Through all eternity.

PART FIVE

In Passing

I can write these poems,
Which you will know are true,
Just once, in passing.
And you who share this fate with me
Will read them
In passing.

But through all the endless generations
Of this incredible miracle,
Know this:
If I had shared your time with you,
I would have loved you
As I have loved these others.

There will be others
Who will share your life and time.
It would make me happy to feel
That I had removed a stone or two
From your pathway
In passing.

You Said

You said,
"My heart boils up inside me."
And you said,
"I have felt for but few men
As I feel for you."

And it is certainly true:
I have felt for but few men
As I feel for you.

Waiting Song

You sailed upon a purple ship
That faded in the afterglow,
And with a prayer upon my lip
I sighed that I had let you go.
I waited on the gleaming shore,
Watched the glimmer of the sea,
Saw the eastern moon that tore
Your quiet love away from me.

One, two, three, four—
I'm passing time away.
A hundred and a million more,
And you will come to stay.
You said you'd come a year ago,
And you will come, my dear, I know.
Five, six, seven, eight—
And I shall wait, and I shall wait.

To Roberta

Words fail me when I see
Your charming ecstasy,
The fire that flickers in your eyes,
Your velvet lips held in surprise,
The lovely grace that lights your face.
My heart grows wide,
I melt inside.
I gaze in rapturous reverie.

Sighs or less to express
The radiance of your loveliness,
The silver bell low in your voice,
The softness of each golden tress,
The breast that makes my own rejoice.
What may I bring,
What praises sing
When voice is stilled by secret stress?

Muses strained, words enchained,
Enchanted beauty unexplained . . .
By your flowing form enrapt,
I leave the source of love untapped.
Perchance the force becoming great
Will bend the dam beneath the weight,
And breaking barrier, bursting free,
Will give my heart fit melody
To praise your charming ecstasy.

I Love You, Bud

I love you, Bud:
You are so lank and lithe,
Your belly so hard and flat,
Your middle so trim.

I love you, Bud:
I love the bright energy
That quickens your step,
The languor that relaxes you,
Your muscles scintillating in action,
The whole of your virile being.

I love you, Bud:
Your eyes black with fire
And soft with love,
The sentiment of your muscular face,
The moisture of your set lips,
The thickness of your jet hair.

I love you, Bud:
Beauty in action,
Force bent to friendship,
Kindliness incarnate,
Youth at crux.

Give Me

Something soft and gay and sweet
In this day of throbbing beat;
Something tender, debonaire,
In this blaring trumpet flare;
Something peaceful and serene
In this now chaotic scene.

Someone simple, good and bright
In this supercharged delight;
Someone honest, clean and strong
In this honkey-tonk ding-dong;
Someone strolling in a wood
In this day of spilling blood.

Give me this, and I'll not care
For the crazy world's despair,
For the gory cry of war
Shaking now our very door,
For the bankrupt generation
Overrunning our nation.

Give me this, and I'll not care
For the madness in the air.

Letter by Sea

I dropped a letter in the sea.
What secret love transported me
My honest thoughts to so express,
My inner self to so undress
That, writing well, my writing failed,
That my confession went unmailed?

I tore the letter twice apart,
For what it carried was my heart,
And ardent things must be concealed,
Silent thoughts be not revealed.
By sea alone what I confessed
Could be received and darkly blessed.

The water washed the words away,
But not the love, for that will stay
Locked in my heart in secrecy,
Guarded through eternity.

Because of This

Because of this
You will remember me,
Just a plain human being,
Because of these simple words.

You will know me because,
Like you, I ate, I slept, I loved,
Because, like you, I sinned—
If it was a sin
To be myself,
And love my love,
And love and love again
As nature prompted me.

Anyway, it was my life
To be myself and love.
And life was fine
And brimming full of happiness;

It brought me comrades
Strong and beautiful
Who gave of their great selves to me,
And you will remember them—and me
Because of this.

You, Cecil

As today, Cecil,
You, a tugboat engineer,
Leaned against the counter
In the country store,
You engraved yourself on my memory:

Sandy-blond hair parted on the side
Cropping out around the white sailor cap
Tossed back on your head,
Swarthy, full, muscular face,
Friendly gray eyes
Crinkling with each genial smile,
Firm lips, even teeth,
Powerful neck.

You, Cecil,
Just leaning there relaxed,
Cordial and smiling,
Meeting my eyes with kindliness;
You,
In starched, spotless clothes,
Gray jacket,
Gray creased trousers,
Colorful socks,
Polished shoes;
Leaning there
With your legs spread apart,
Your clothes not hiding you,
Not hiding the youth of you,
The fullness of you,
The power of you,
Your big chest,
Rugged waist,
Stocky arms above veined hands,
Parted legs swelling crisp trousers
With muscular undulations.

You, full of force, full of warmth.
You talking quietly
In gentle voice
About tugboat experiences.
You smiling,

Glancing lovingly
From one to another,
Marking yourself down perpetually
In every man, woman and child,
Perpetually in me,
And, through these words,
Perpetually in history.

You, Cecil!

So Many Times

So many times,
Capable of giving,
Capable of receiving,
Capable of giving and receiving,
Sharing, reciprocating,
I have gone on
Overfull,
Empty,
Or both overfull and empty,
Lonely,
Without you.

So many times,
The charge has had no recipient,
The receptacle has had no charge,
Reciprocity has gone unfulfilled,
When, perhaps,
You too
Have been alone and lonely.

So many times,
Because of the ignorance of man,

95

The stupid tabus,
The primitive traditions,
The false judgments, half-truths, fears, and hates,
The essential mission of life
Has been obstructed, impeded, or delayed.
Beauty has been driven
Into hiding,
And, in one, life has throbbed on massively
Without fulfillment,
While another
Has languished in the bitterness
Of lonely longing and yearning
Even to the point of death.
Millions have died for lack of love.

So many times,
Without you,
I have wondered at the miracle
Of magnificent energy
With no place to go,
Or at the void of deficiency
Without energy to fill it,
Or at the paradox
Of explosive power
And simultaneous yearning
Without you, the answerer,
To start the perpetual rotation.

So many times,
And even now,
And even now again,
Though you are absent,
I love you, need you,
Call to you again.

The Music Has Ceased

The music has ceased
And the unknown musician has vanished;
Never will he know
How I languish here,
Steeped in beauty,
Permeated by his melody.
The music has ceased.
The unknown musician has vanished
And he will never know. . . .

Celebration

At Rambouillet
Near Paris
Is art that needs celebrating,
Uncelebrated.
All who see it
Are moved to profound depths
By its truth.
For art is truth,
As everybody knows.
Yet nobody speaks.

A friend said,
"There are two kinds of love:
Love of man for man
And love of man for woman."
There are more kinds of love than that:
A multitude of loves
With an infinity of heights and depths,
A different love for every creature.

But my friend was reaching out
For the truth.

A Greek said,
"Females are for children,
Males for pleasure."
But all love is bliss.

Anyway,
At the Grotto of Love,
The boat landing at the head
Of the formal pools of Rambouillet,
Truth stands stark in sculpture.

To the right
A perfect and powerful man
Holds
In reclining embrace
A shapely woman.

To the left
A handsome male
Holds his clean-muscled comrade
In affectionate encirclement.

The second mates
Are fit companions to the first.

Who shall celebrate the lovers
Of the Grotto of Love,
The loveliest lovers in sculpture?

Far away on the China Sea,
High in the stratosphere,
Their image is engraved
In silent hearts.

This is our day
Of celebration.

Song of Evening

When the sun in golden glory
Cools its flame in western sea
And the gulls their wheeling story
Shriek in trailing rhapsody,
Then still I lie upon the beach
As clouds parade their colors by,
And toward the fading sky I reach
While one by one the stars reply.

When palms with swaying fingers sketch
Their outlines on the glowing west
And one last boat with sails a-stretch
Bows low to wave in homeward quest,
Then lie I yet upon the shore
As night clouds draw their veil a-pace,
And starlit heavens I implore
While answer comes from sparkling space.

When moon in radiant aura peers
Above its secret forest lair
And silhouetted palm tree hears
A night bird sing his song somewhere,
Still linger I upon the strand
As silver clouds traverse the sky,
And give the jeweled arc command
While pallid moonlight makes reply.

Loneliness at Night

We lay there lonely under stars,
Starlight dancing in the spray,
Lay there lingering midst the spars
And wreckage set by storms astray.
The night was warm and passionate.
The palms mad music sang.
And summer sent her opiate
To strike through magic fang.

Silent lay we on the sand,
Desert stretching soullessly,
Together close upon the strand
That relics bore of treachery.
Voiceless lay we through the night,
Sleepless, open-eyed,
Till dawn had put the dark to flight,
And lonely still, we sighed.

Love Knows One Law

Love knows one law:
Love is considerate.
Love puts others first
In work, in play, in love.
. Love may do
What one does not personally wish
For the happiness of another.
But love does not ask
What another does not wish to give.
Love may surrender,
Never force;

May give,
Never take.

True love knows no limits.
Love will sacrifice
Name and honor,
Fortune,
Life itself
For love.

Death
To the lover
Comes easy.
Life is love's highest gift.

With such love
In all mankind
What happiness will be denied,
What urge unfulfilled,
What arms empty,
What urgent impulse checked,
What pulsing loins unemptied,
What fainting spirit
Unreplenished,
Unsustained?

Love is the answer
To all the pains, tortures and frustrations,
To all the heartaches
Of human life.

Love's Discovery

I never dreamed
That such a pure and moving love
Could come.
I never found such tender peace
With any former mate.
I never thought
That love could be so great.
I misjudged you,
Comparing yours with loves I knew before.
But early standards do not hold for you.
All doubts arising from betrayals past
Prove false, and you alone prove true.

My faith in man had long ago worn thin.
I wondered then if I alone of men
Kept trust.
But you have healed my aching heart,
My bleeding wounds,
And believe in you I must.

Still,
Who can say how long this ecstasy will last?
Tides and storms today are running fast.
And yet,
Of this, my love, I have no doubt:
You alone I cannot do without.
A day with you is worth a lifetime with another mate.
Who would believe
That love could be so great?

You are the affirmation of all truth.
I am convinced of this.
You fill my spirit fresher yet with youth,
And love's fulfillment grows with every kiss.
You are thus my first, my only fate.
I never knew that love could be so great.

Silver Night

A silver ship in a silver sea
And hardly a stir at all,
A drooping sail and an idle wheel
And a lazy lift and fall,
The hot air of a heavy night
And a song for you and me:
No silver night is idle, lad,
When we are off at sea.

Man Mystery

Man is a mystery
Which I cannot hope to solve.
Perhaps if I had been born
A thousand generations later
I might understand some things
About man
Which puzzle me.
As it is,
For nearly thirty years I have tried
And cannot yet explain
The wonder of man.

All I know
Is that I have lived
And enjoyed the miracle of life.
Maybe I have been mistaken
When I thought I was right.
Maybe some of the things
I thought wrong
And suffered for

ere not wrong after all.
The future may say
That I was merely shattering old tabus:
Tabus so strong that they almost shattered me.

At any rate,
Mistakenly or unmistakenly,
I have loved.
I have loved man and men
And woman and women
And children
And all living things
And life itself
Platonically
And unplatonically.
I have loved them all
With admiration
And fascination
And surging energy
That broke all bonds of restraint.

Clif, for example.
Clif is a riverman,
A crabman and an oysterman.
He steers his boat out into the dark
And back through the storm,
And out into the twilight
And back through the moonlight.
He is burnt brown.
He is salty.
He is tall.
He is bulky and brawny.
He has the force of the sun
And the power to cope with the sea itself.

Clif is married.
His wife is small and blonde.

She has a blond male child.
The three of them
Live in a two-room shack
In a pine forest
Beside the Pamlico River.
Clif built the shack himself.

Upon such homes
Rests the future of humanity.

Anyway,
I love Clif
And his life.
I love his family
And the kind of people they are.
I embrace them all.

And Clif loves me.
I know that.
He and Frank
Once started to build me a house.
They got as far as the foundation.
They hewed timbers with an axe
Out of pine saplings.
I finished the house
In my imagination.

Of such is the marvel of man.

Then Dan.
In a poem I called him Ananioski.
That was his Indian name.
His poem speaks for him.
The memory of his massive emission
Revitalizes me even now.

My thanks are in this poem.

The fabric of these thirty years.
The travels.
The meeting of people.
Negroes.
I slept with them and loved them.
Adolphe in Paris,
My mulatto roommate from Martinique.
He was on leave
From the French Foreign Legion.
He loved women,
But he loved me too:
He was bubbling over with love.
He was tall and muscular,
Lithe and electric,
An atomic dynamo.
I shall not forget Adolphe.

Then Kato,
The Jap who loved me.
And Okano,
The Jap whom I loved.
When they were on lookout
On the forecastle head
Of the Ginyo Maru
We looked at the phosphorescent streaks
Made by the sharks
Dashing across the bow
Near Singapore.

Then Rao,
The Hindu doctor
With whom I saw the pyramids
On a moonlit night.
And another Rao,
Law student at Bombay University.
We swam together in Back Bay
And at Juhu Beach.

Clif the riverman,
Dan the Cherokee,
Adolphe the mulatto,
Okano the Jap,
The two Raos:
They tied my world into a unity.
Loving them
I loved all men everywhere,
Embraced them all
As comrades and brothers,
Loved them beyond bounds.

And women?
I am the son
Of a million generations
Of women.

Writing this
I must not forget Whitman,
The greatest American poet,
Who loved all the men and women
Who make America,
Who united a great continental nation.
The world will never forget
That great lover,
Whitman.
I cannot forget him here.
I must carry his meaning
To all the world.

Ah friend!
If I were great enough
To be this moment everywhere,
To be in every home,
And on every ship,
And in the theatres,

In the chancelleries,
And on the battlefields
In all the armies
On both sides of every war,
How good it would be
To embrace every human being,
Every aged person
And every infant,
Every youth
And all men, women and children,
And to love them all
With a close personal love.

For certainly I am everybody's friend:
Hitler's and Stalin's
Tojo's and Roosevelt's;
The friend of every coal miner and farmer,
Of every waitress,
Of every brothel keeper and convict,
Of every woodchopper
And of every drunkard:
All they need
Is to serve one another
And to love.

Those who are apart
I would draw together;
And those who are down
I would lift up
To view the broad and universal beauty of life:
The wonder of man.

Nobody need fear me.
I cannot inflict a mortal wound.
Love cannot wound at all.
All men may come to me.
One is as welcome as the other.

Men living are welcome
And men dead are welcome.
Those yet unborn are welcome.
And all are welcome.
More than welcome:
Urgently desired.

Whoever you are,
I love you,
And I want you to love me,
And all of us
To love one another
Without restraint
And without bounds.

Nearing thirty
I cannot explain man.
I can only say
That he is marvelous.
That his body and mind and soul
Are beautiful
And capable of unprecedented achievement,

Capable of moulding the earth
And mastering it,
Of bringing happiness and abundant love
To everyone,
And of undertaking
A great pioneering
Into the universe.

Man of the past,
Comrades living and about me,
Sons unborn,
I must say you are a mystery
Unfolding infinite mystery.

But you are great.
You are wonderful.
You yourself,
Who cannot conquer yourself,
Are the great conqueror of the universe.
I salute you!

Some Day

Some day,
Not asking why or how,
Nature's sweetest gifts
Man will allow,
And to love's drift
He will bow.

Some day,
And may that day be soon!
In our bold rehearsal
We shall find the tune,
With love universal
We shall swoon.

Some day
Man will learn
Not to yearn.
What nature generated
Was her intent,
And what she motivated
She meant.

Two Sofas

There were two sofas
On the veranda.

Today we leaned in the breeze
On one sofa together.
I did not dare touch you.
We talked of laziness.

You went away,
But soon returned
And stretched out
On the other sofa.
"There's a bed for each of us,"
You said.

One bed for two of us
Was what I wanted.

And perhaps you too wanted
One bed for two of us.
How could I know?
And how could you know?
And who would dare tell?

Perhaps some day
There will be urgency and impulse,
Throb and abatement.
And again urgency.

Two Teacups

This morning two teacups
Were on the table,
One from which I had lately drunk
And another.

For quite a while I looked
At the cup across the table.
I picked it up,
Touched its lip to my lip
And caught, I think,
The aroma of a sweeter tea.

The half-cup of tea
Was still warm.
It tasted mildly sweet
And of lemon.
I sipped it slowly.

That was one thing.

Then,
After wandering around the room a bit,
I lay down.

Not my pillow,
But the one on the far side of the bed,
Attracted me.
I rolled over to it,
Buried my nose in it,
And breathed, I think,
The loveliest perfume.

This morning I did some strange things,
For you had just gone.

Your Personality

You are not like Hercules, Atlas, or Sampson.
You have a neat body,
Slightly muscular.
The veins in your forearms
Show that blood courses through you.
You have creases in your cheeks,
A shock of sandy hair,
Pleasant gray eyes
With unassuming crinkles of geniality
That are neither notable nor dramatic.
You make no effort to impress,
Yet you impress.

There are certain ripples of expression
On your kindly face,
A certain bearing in your gestures,
That mark the difference
Between you and another.

Altogether,
You suggest the sincere and modest love
That wells from the depths of your being.
Not muscles, not proportions, not looks—
Though you look well enough—
Distinguish you.

Your charm seems to flow
From some inward source,
From that elusive and insubstantial thing:
Your personality.

The Sodomite

Once, in Southold, Long Island,
A Presbyterian minister,
Whose name not even God remembers,
Organized a movement
To run a local schoolmaster
Out of town.

The schoolmaster was charged
With having romantic relations
With local school boys.

The school was thereafter called Sodom,
Those who attended the school, Sodomites,
And the school itself was soon abandoned.

Now, on Long Island,
The birthplace of this beloved schoolmaster
Is a shrine,
Statues are erected to his memory,
And magnificent schools
Are named for this immortal Sodomite,
Walt Whitman.

What More Can Be Said About Love?

What more can be said about love?
So much has been said already.
All the generations have talked about it.
Books, songs and secret nights
Have been filled with it.
Each youth has shared his strength

At its altar.
And yet
Love is always fresh and full.

Other Nights of Stars

My dearest,
I want to tell you a story.

It happened on a dark night.
There was no moon.
Silently they stood there together,
He and she.
He wanted to tell her that she was beautiful.
The words caught deep in his throat.

He felt her fingers
Tremulous
Upon his arm.
Underneath the cypress trees
Beside the sparkling lake
He and she were together
And out of the world.

He touched her body.
It was soft as velvet.
Her hair was blowing in the breeze.
Behind them were the woods,
Dark and lonely.
And in the sky
The stars were shining,
And in the water.

(Hear the owl, my dearest.
How solitary he sounds
In the distance.
But we are here together.
This night of stars is ours.)

He spoke softly
Telling her of stars and night,
Enclosing her in his arms.
And standing there beside the lake
Under the stars,
He kissed her.

(Spanish moss swaying from black cypress,
Stars shooting in sky and water.
How gently blows the breeze.)

But, my dearest,
Here the story is sad.
She was afraid.
Breaking from his arms,
She ran breathlessly away.
Was it the stars in the sky?
The stars in the water?
The stars in his eyes?
The night?

(Perhaps we do not know,
You and I.
The Spanish moss is still swaying.
Innocent of all but our nearness,
Our hearts beat breast to breast.)

All moments pass,
(Even as this moment is passing.)
Separately they went their ways
Each yearning for the other.

No longer shone the stars
In the sky and in the water.

But, my dearest,
Let us rejoice!
The story is not ended.
The lake is there
And the stars are there.
Tonight is a night of stars.
Perhaps they will find tonight
The beauty that passed unseen,
The joy that slipped unfelt.

(Even now, your lips.)

That Was Not Love

Though you were as lovely
As any maiden
Who ever walked through a cornfield,
Though your hair was as silken
As golden
And curled to your shoulders,
Though your blue eyes
Were flecked with gold
And your sunny lips
Were as soft as velvet,
That was not love.

Though my arms embraced you,
Mistakenly,
And I felt the firm pressure
Of your breasts
Against my chest,

117

Though our bodies
Met as a line
And we pressed our lips together,
That was not love.

Though my comrades,
Whom I loved,
Envied me,
And you were the most desired lass
In the countryside,
Though you would have brought pride
To any lover's heart
In any company,
And though I have not seen your equal
Among women,
That was not love.

Such is the irony of life
That you loved me
Who did not love you.

God Is Love

God is love,
And what is love but caring,
You for me, me for you,
Comradeship and sharing?

God is love,
Not of sword and saber,
But brotherhood and fellowship,
Neighbor's love for neighbor.

God is love,
And what thing can be dearer
Than you for me, me for you,
Near and growing nearer?

God is love,
The urgent joy of giving,
The good that conquers hate and fear,
The dawn of happy living.

God is love,
The warmth of friendly caring,
You for me, me for you,
Equality and sharing.

To My Brothers

To my brothers let me say this:
Lament not.
Life is not gloomy or serious
If you are courageous and free.
Live your life and enjoy it,
For life is glorious.
Come forth and proclaim yourself,
And life is triumphant.
Be fearless and live,
For of idleness and repression
Are fear and despair.

Are you different?
Are you alone?
Then proclaim yourself,
For you are of the earth,
Born of the earth,
Bred of the earth
And part of the earth.

To share the sunshine,
The sea spray,
The joy and lightness of the earth,
Is your birthright.

Are you different?
Are you alone?
Then proclaim yourself.
There are millions different,
Millions alone.
Announce yourself,
And the grass that grows on the pathway
Will be beaten down
By a thousand footsteps.

PART SIX

A mon ami

Jamais tu sauras comment tu es cher.
Pour moi tu es bon ami et frère,
Toujours camarade, toujours confrère.
Mais, mon ami, jamais tu sauras
Comment doucement je pense à toi,
Comment je veux toute la journée
Constamment être à ton coté.
Si, mon ami, si tu savais,
Tu serais également un ami pour moi.
Mais comment tu es cher jamais tu sauras.

A ma chérie

Si j'avais un lac d'encre,
Ma chérie,
Je pourrais écrire un peu
De l'amour que je possède pour toi;
Car tu es l'ange de tous mes rèves
Et le désespoir de tout mon coeur.

Quand les ombres de la nuit,
Ma chérie,
Obscurcissent l'aspect de ma fenêtre,
Je regarde la naissance des étoiles
Me souvenant de l'éclair de tes yeux;

Et le velours bleu du ciel
Me fait songer
A la douceur de tes seins.

Je t'aime, ma chérie,
Mais tout seul à ma fenêtre
Je suis. . . .

Jamais

Jamais vous pourriez,
Vous ne pourriez jamais
Savoir
Comment
Quand vous refusez l'amour
Que, de tout mon coeur,
Je vous offre,
Que
Quand vous me repoussez
Vos doigts me paraissent des poignards
Qui me percent
Coeur et âme.
Si je pouvais—
Hélas, si je pouvais—
J'empêcherais l'amour
Qui me vole ma paix du jour
Et mon sommeil de la nuit.
Je ne veux pas vous aimer.
Je veux échapper à la torture.
Mais je vous aime.

Mon amour est une flamme
Qui s'éteindra
Quand il n'y aura plus rien brûler,
Quand il n'y aura plus mon coeur.

Souvenir de Louis

Corps à corps,
Coeur à coeur,
L'ami que j'aime
Et moi.
Main à main,
Chaleur à chaleur,
Tout que j'aime
Est toi.

Qui sait le monde?
Qui sait future?
Qui sait que vient demain?
L'amitié est profonde.
L'amour est bien sûr
Quand nous sommes main à main.

Toujours l'amitié,
Toujours l'amour
De toi, camarade,
Et moi.
Coté à coté
Toujours et toujours,
A toi, camarade!
A toi!

Souvenir de toi

Quand je veux oublier, je me souviens
De la douceur de ta voix,
Car l'oiseau chantant à ma fenêtre
Doucement chante comme toi,

Et le parfum du printemps naissant
Est ton parfum pour moi.

Dans la rue je vais pour oublier
Le rouge de tes lèvres velours,
Mais le soleil mourant,
Comme tes lèvres, brûlant,
Hante la fin du jour.

Vient la nuit. Encore je marche
Desirant oublier,
Mais la lune argent
Est comme tes cheveux,
Les étoiles sont comme tes yeux.

J'écoute la chanson du vent, des feuilles,
Et pense à ta robe satin.
Mais tu es cause de toute ma soif
Et cause de toute ma faim.

Quand je veux oublier, je me souviens
De la douceur de ta voix,
Car l'oiseau chantant à ma fenêtre
Doucement chante comme toi.

Afterthought

At this twilight of parting
Before farewell I say
Be kind to one another
In work, in love, in play.
To sow love
Is to reap love,

To bestow love
Is to grow love, to keep love.

I love you, friend,
So please
Be reckless with allowances,
Sparing with prohibitions,
Generous with kindnesses,
Stingy with judgments,
Prodigal with love,
Delinquent with hate,
Abundant with consideration, boundless with forgiveness
          and infinite with affection.

Freely give love, freely receive love.
If you are overcharged,
Do not waste your energy.
Think of those who faint.
Discharge yourself on the undercharged.
If you are strong,
Seek the weak,
And if you are weak,
Do not shrink from the strong.
Welcome the strong, receive the strong, embrace the strong,
          respond to the shock of the strong.

All people are different,
And all loves are different.
No matter how different your friend's love,
Honor it.
The things forbidden that continue
Were meant to continue.
They were nature's safety valves.
The trouble grew
Of forbidding them.

Do not challenge the magnetisms of nature
In yourself or anyone.
Impediment is painful.
Frustration produces discord and terror.
Mutual desire is the essence of the argument.
Nature knows best.
Out of miasmic unconsciousness
We grew to consciousness
By nature's guidance.
Love knows her own way.

Help each to find his heart's desire.
Love the love of others
As your own love.
Wherever there is weakness
Help strength to find it.
Then
When you are weak
Love will bolster you up.
You yourself
Will know love's electronics,
Love's rejuvenation.

So always look to love,
Never back to hate.
Be kind to one another
And kindness is your fate.

Prayer for No Answer

Who are you fiends
Who would drop
Atomic bombs on thousands?

These are people
You would kill:
Sparkling eyes,
Moving muscles,
Laughter,
Joyous life within.

That kid
With wide blue eyes
And golden ringlets;
That little girl
With straw-colored hair
Hanging straight like straw.
Say,
That imp
With the sharp chin
And olive skin,
Dark eyes dancing,
Trusting you to keep them living.

Who are you fiends
Who would drop
Atomic bombs on children?
These are children
You would kill,
Looking at you
With trusting eyes of love.

No such fiends, I pray.
Be the answer silence.